# FBA and BIP

## Functional Behavioral Assessment & Behavior Intervention Plan

Designed to assist educators in using Functional Behavioral Assessments (FBAs) to develop successful Behavior Intervention Plans (BIPs) for students with behavior problems, this reference guide presents an overview of their components and provides concrete steps for effective implementation. FBAs and BIPs are best viewed as a single, continuous process rather than two separate procedures.

## What is Positive Behavioral Interventions and Supports (PBIS)?

PBIS is a proactive approach to support positive student behavior and create healthy learning environments that enhances teaching and learning. PBIS organizes evidence-based behavioral practices and systems into a continuum in which students experience supports based on their needs.

Much like Response To Intervention (RTI) which focuses primarily on providing academic/instructional support, PBIS follows a three-tiered prevention system. At Tier 1, all students receive supports in order to prevent behavior problems and teach pro-social behaviors. If the behavior of individual students is not responsive, more targeted behavioral supports are provided at Tier 2. Students requiring more intensive and/or highly individualized supports are served at Tier 3.

### Designing School-Wide Systems for Student Success

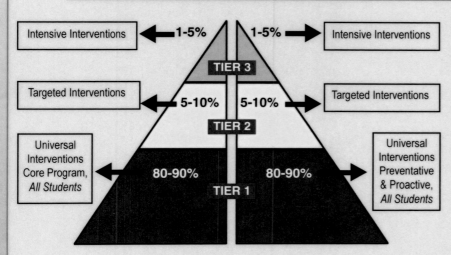

**The Relationship between PBIS and FBA-BIP**

PBIS is a system that provides a framework of positive behavior supports for all students.

With school-wide and classroom supports in place, most students' behavioral needs are addressed. However, some students will require a higher level of intervention. For these students, the FBA-BIP is an effective tool. FBA-BIP is an individualized, evidence-based process that is useful for any student (general education or special education) when behavior is interfering with his/her learning. sometimes a student may appear to require an FBA-BIP when, perhaps, schools need to develop a well-implemented system of positive behavioral supports.

**TIP: Remember to check federal guidelines and your state mandates which indicate when an FBA-BIP is required.**

schools face an increasing number of students whose behavior interferes with the success of daily classroom instruction. Fortunately, are usually able to rely on positive behavioral supports, solid teaching practices, clear rules and expectations, and praise which encourages behaviors. However, these strategies may fail to help some students improve their behavior and may actually worsen an already difficult For these students, the use of the process known as FBA/BIP to develop positive behavior intervention plans is essential.

## What are the Basic Beliefs About Behavior?

- ehavior serves a purpose or "function", such as "gaining attention" or "avoiding tasks"
- ehavior is related to the context (where and under what conditions it occurs)
- ehavior is a complex response to a dynamic relationship between many variables: people, places, and events
- If the positive behaviors expected from students are taught, the amount, frequency and intensity of problem behavior can be decreased or minimized(Positive Behavior Support Model)
- If a problem behavior can be defined, explained and predicted, there is a likelihood that it can be prevented

## What is an FBA?

An FBA is a problem-solving process for understanding and ultimately addressing student problem behaviors. It relies on a variety of techniques and strategies to identify the purpose or function of specific behavior. Designed to help teams select interventions that directly address the problem behavior, its focus is on identifying significant, student-specific social, affective, cognitive, and/or environmental factors associated with the occurrence (and non-occurrence) of specific behaviors. This broad perspective offers a better understanding of the purpose behind student behavior. An FBA looks beyond the behavior itself and:

- Is based on the field of applied behavior analysis;
- Involves a systematic process for gathering information about "why" a behavior is occurring which leads to the development of a BIP;
- Is designed to help determine relationships between the environment and problem behavior;
- Leads to more specific and effective interventions.

**Several Advantages of using FBAs to deal with behavior problems:**

- Considers individual differences and environmental factors in the development of behavior support plans;
- Directly and logically links intervention(s) to the problem behavior;
- Increases treatment effectiveness.

## What is a BIP?

A Behavior Intervention Plan (BIP) is:

- Derived as product from the information gathered during the FBA process;
- Developed after collecting sufficient information about a student's behavior to determine the likely function of that behavior;
- Focused on the prevention of the problem behavior, as well as the teaching of alternative/replacement behaviors;
- Based on an understanding of "why" a student is having difficulties which is extremely useful in addressing a wide range of problem behaviors.

**TIP**: FBAs and BIPs should be viewed as a unit. FBA data informs the development and re-evaluation of the BIP. The FBA-BIP process refers to a systematic approach to identifying and changing behavior by manipulating the antecedents (things that happen before) and the consequences (things that happen after) the behavior.

# 6 Steps for Conducting the FBA-BIP Process

## Step #1: Identifying and Defining the Problem Behaviors

Step #1 is to identify the problem behavior. Beginning work should include developing a profile of the student's strengths and needs. Awareness of these strengths and needs will help the team determine intervention goals, as well as specific intervention ideas.

**TIP**: Areas in which a student excels often helps develop a positive behavior intervention plan that works. By understanding and incorporating a student's strengths into the plan, a positive behavior momentum is created. When a student experiences a number of successes, positive momentum builds and he/she is more likely to engage in positive behaviors.

### Developing a Behavioral Support Team

During Step #1 it is important to identify the team members who will be involved in the FBA-BIP process. The team should be trans-disciplinary, including members such as a classroom teacher (general and/or special education), a pupil services staff member (school psychologist, social worker or guidance counselor), a related service provider (as appropriate), an administrator, the parent and the student (if practical). This process is most effective when implemented as a collaborative effort.

**TIP**: Involve the student in this process if at all possible. It is better to do something "with" rather than "to" the student.

### Defining the Problem Behavior

As part of Step #1, a specific problem behavior must be identified. It should be operationally defined in observable and measurable terms (i.e., gets out of his seat, bites another student, calls out in class).

Avoid the use of constructs such as hostile, disrespectful, and noncompliant. These terms are not clearly definable. Be specific and define behavior by what the student does or doesn't do, what the student says and/or how the student acts.

| Instead of…. | Define behavior as…. |
|---|---|
| Disruptive | Making inappropriate comments in class |
| Aggressive | Hitting other students with his/her fists |
| Disrespectful | Cursing at the teacher |
| Distractible | Not completing tasks on time |

**TIP**: Description of behavior should pass the "stranger test," meaning, someone not familiar with the student should be able to read the description of the student's problem behavior and understand it. What behaviors would they "see" or "hear?"

*Any definition of problem behaviors should include:*

- What the problem behavior looks and sounds like? (description)
- How often the problem behavior occurs? (frequency)
- How long the problem behavior lasts when it occurs? (duration)
- How disruptive or dangerous the problem behaviors are? (intensity)

## Step #2: Gathering Information

Effective intervention is based on a comprehensive understanding of the variables and circumstances influencing the behavior. Data collection can include a combination of indirect and direct methods, and must represent information from multiple perspectives and across a range of different settings, activities, and situations. Gathering data should be a

...continued on next page

Consequences fall into two basic categories. Things that students:
(1) "Get" as a result of a behavior (peer attention, teacher attention, good grades and/or high scores, food and/or drink);
(2) "Avoid or get out of" as result of the behavior (difficult work, being asked to do something, social situations, classwork and/or homework);

## Guiding Questions:
- What happens to the student after the behavior?
- Does the environment change as a result of the behavior?
- What is gained or lost?
- How do others respond to the behavior?

## Functions of Behavior:
All behaviors serve a purpose (function) for the individual and are strengthened or reinforced by the environment. The purpose or function is not necessarily a conscious decision by the student. Functions of behavior can be divided into "Getting" or "Avoiding" certain things:

|  | Demand/ Activity | Attention | Tangible (object) | Sensory/Physical |
|---|---|---|---|---|
| Get |  |  |  |  |
| Avoid |  |  |  |  |

## Examples of Behavior Function:

| Behavior | Consequence | Function |
|---|---|---|
| Makes inappropriate comments | Work removed | Avoid demands |
| Does not complete work | Teacher redirection | Get teacher attention |
| Hits peers | Computer time to calm down | Get preferred activities |

## Example of a Behavior Summary Statement:

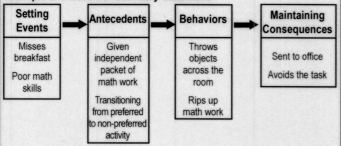

The Five Outcomes of the FBA Process:
1. A clear description of the problem behaviors.
2. Direct Observation data
3. Situations, events, and times that predict when behaviors will and will not occur (i.e., setting events and antecedents)
4. Consequences that maintain the problem behaviors (function)
5. A Behavior Summary Statement

**TIP:** In rare instances, a Functional Analysis (FA) is used to test a Summary Statement/Hypothesis by systematically manipulating the antecedents or consequences.

# Step #4: Developing a Behavior Intervention Plan (BIP)

After collecting sufficient information about a student's behavior to complete the Summary Statement and determine the likely function of that behavior, the BIP is developed. A well-developed Summary

Statement provides the foundation for effective individualized positive BIPs that focus on:
- Preventing antecedents that trigger problem behavior
- Teaching appropriate alternative behaviors
- Modifying consequences that maintain the problem behavior and including consequences that reinforce alternative/desired behavior

**TIP:** It is much easier to change the environment (setting events, antecedents, and consequences) than change the student.

## Antecedent Strategies:
- Replicate antecedents that trigger SUCCESS for the student.
- Change antecedents that trigger the problem behavior.
- Examples of Antecedent Strategies include:
    —Putting tape to indicate where the students line up
    —Using music or timers to signal transitions
    —Reducing the number of problems on a page
    —Allowing choice for individual or group projects
    —Using visual supports for activities and behavior expectations (in order to decrease verbal prompts)

**TIP:** Use antecedent strategies as a proactive strategy rather than relying only on consequences as a reactive approach to affect behavior.

## Teach Appropriate Alternative/Replacement Behaviors
Behaviors that achieve the same function as the problem behavior are called alternative behaviors (functionally equivalent replacement behaviors). Consider using a stepping stone between the problem behavior and the ultimate desired behavior. For example:
**Problem behavior:** hits peers
**Alternative behavior:** takes a break
**Desired behavior:** keeps hands to self

The alternative behavior must....
- Satisfy same function (purpose) of the problem behavior
- Be in the student's repertoire
- Be more reinforcing for the student
- Be age/culturally appropriate

## Example of Alternative Behaviors:

|  | Demand/ Activity | Attention | Tangible (object) | Sensory/Physical |
|---|---|---|---|---|
| Get | Request specific activity | Gain attention in appropriate ways | Ask for object | Request sensory activity |
| Avoid | Request a break | Communicate needs (I need some time alone.) | Communicate needs (I do not like to touch that.) | Communicate needs (It is too loud) |

## Putting it all Together:

| Behavior | Consequence | Function | Alternative Behaviors |
|---|---|---|---|
| Makes inappropriate comments | Work removed | Avoid of task demand | Requests break at a table in the back of the classroom |
| Does not complete work | Teacher re-direction | Gain teacher attention | Requests assistance from teacher |

The BIP needs to include Behavior Teaching Strategies:
- What skill does the student need to learn?
- How will the new alternative behavior be taught and reinforced?

...continued on next page

Determine whether problem results from a Skill or Performance Deficit (or both).

*Skill deficit (Can't do)...*student does not know how to perform the skill. If the student has a skill deficit, specific strategies must be implemented to teach the skill. Examples of skill deficits include: asking for help, following directions, or problem solving.

*Performance deficit (Won't do)...*student can perform a skill but does not use it consistently (i.e., in particular setting), the student must practice the skill in a different setting (generalizing the skill). The BIP should increase motivation through reinforcement.

> TIP: BIPs that focus on teaching skills will be more effective than plans that serve to control behavior. Interventions based upon control often fail to generalize and usually serve only to suppress behavior. This results in the student manifesting unaddressed needs in new inappropriate ways.

## Modifying Consequences

- What is the response when alternative/desired behavior occurs? (positive reinforcers)
- What is the response when problem behavior occurs? (negative consequences)
- Remember to change the maintaining consequence in order to stop inadvertently reinforcing the problem behavior

## Positive Reinforcement—presentation of something rewarding immediately following a behavior, making it more likely that the behavior will occur in the future. It is one of the most powerful tools for shaping or changing behavior. The reinforcement must be strong enough to change the behavior.

When first introducing a reinforcer, it must be immediate, frequent and continuous. Use differential reinforcement for new or difficult tests. Differential reinforcement means that reinforcement is provided for behaviors when these behaviors occur at certain times and places, whereas reinforcement is not provided when the behaviors do not occur during other times and places. Use incremental reinforcement to reinforce small behavioral steps in order to shape behavior.

Effective consequences should be:
- As small as possible and/or paired with natural reinforcers
- Made part of routines and systems
- Pre-planned and taught
- A greater "payoff" to defeat the function of the problem behavior

## Behavior Intervention Planning

All areas of the Behavior Summary Statement must be addressed, for example:

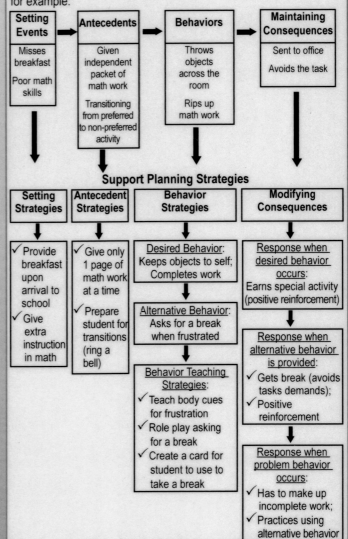

## Step #5: Implementing the BIP

The BIP should identify person(s) responsible for its implementation. However, it must be consistently implemented by all staff members working with the student. A good BIP will fit naturally within the structure of the classroom and school in which it is implemented. The most important factors contributing to effective implementation of BIP are the team members' commitment, capacity and concern for the student. Allow adequate time for complete implementation of the BIP. Remember, not only does the BIP require the student to change his/her behavior, but it also requires the school staff to change their behavior as well.

## Behavior Intervention Plan

| Tasks | Person(s) Responsible | By When | Review Date | Evaluation Decision • Monitor • Modify • Discontinue |
|---|---|---|---|---|
|  |  |  |  |  |
|  |  |  |  |  |
|  |  |  |  |  |
|  |  |  |  |  |
|  |  |  |  |  |

> TIP: Often the problem behavior gets worse (frequency and/or intensity) before it improves.

collaborative process and not the responsibility of only one team member. The data should be collected and analyzed to become the basis for the BIP, and subsequently as a determinant of its effectiveness.

## Indirect Methods:

*Reviewing Records*—provide insights into factors that may have or are currently affecting the student's behavior (i.e., medical or medication issues, family changes---parents separation or divorce).

*Interviews*—provide information from multiple perspectives and help identify variables influencing the behavior. It is essential to interview at least one teacher currently working with the student. Interviews should include open-ended questions about student's strengths and weaknesses, information about when and during what activities the student has difficulties, as well as questions about what the student is doing well. Depending on age, developmental and cognitive levels, the student should be interviewed to obtain his/her perspective about the behavior. Students may identify events that staff miss (e.g., a student is irritable because of missing breakfast). Parent interviews are useful in gathering yet another perspective about the behavior.

## Direct Methods:

Direct observations should occur in the student's natural environment. Data should be collected in various settings and at various times in order to discern a recognizable pattern.

1. **A-B-C Recording** (**A**ntecedent-**B**ehavior-**C**onsequence):
   • The problem **B**ehavior, as well as the time it was initiated and the time it ended is recorded;
   • Activities and events preceding the behavior (**A**ntecedents) are identified;
   • Events that follow the behavior (**C**onsequences) are recorded;
   • Patterns among the **A**ntecedents and the **B**ehavior and the **C**onsequences are identified (see Step # 3).

## An Example:

| Date | Time Behavior Started | Antecedent | Behavior | Consequence | Time Behavior Ended |
|------|------------------------|------------|----------|-------------|----------------------|
| 3/2 | 8:35 | Transition from computer to math | Kicked chair, threw book across the room | Sent to office (missed math) | 8:42 |
| 3/4 | 8:40 | Given math packet for the unit to begin completing | . Ripped up packet, threw it on the floor, threw book, left the room | Sent to office (missed math), Lunch detention-Note home | 9:02 |

**TIP:** Patterns of behaviors are determined by reviewing data over a period of time. Common patterns include days of the week, time of day, schedule of classes, type of activity, staff present, and students present.

2. **Scatter Plot**
   • Records the occurrence and nonoccurrence of behavior across the day to provide a visual display of patterns
   • Suggests possible ways to change the environment to prevent problem behavior and promote alternative/desired behavior).

## An Example:

| Problem Behavior: Throwing objects = | | | | | | |
|---------|----------|-----|-----|-----|-----|-----|
| Time | Activity | 3/2 | 3/3 | 3/4 | 3/5 | 3/6 |
| 8:00 | Arrival | | | | | |
| 8:30 | Math | ▓ | | ▓ | ▓ | |
| 9:15 | Reading | | | | | ▓ |
| 10:00 | P.E. | | | | | |

# Step #3:
# Generating a Summary Statement

Using the information gathered, the team analyzes the data to identify patterns or trends about the student's behavior. The Summary Statement/Hypothesis is your best guess about why the behavior is occuring. It predicts the general conditions under which the behavior is most likely to occur, as well as the probable consequences that may serve to maintain it. During Step #3, the team completes a Behavior Summary Statement.

## Behavior Summary Statement

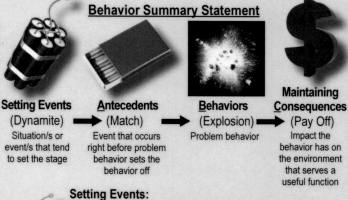

| Setting Events (Dynamite) | Antecedents (Match) | Behaviors (Explosion) | Maintaining Consequences (Pay Off) |
|---|---|---|---|
| Situation/s or event/s that tend to set the stage | Event that occurs right before problem behavior sets the behavior off | Problem behavior | Impact the behavior has on the environment that serves a useful function |

**Setting Events:**
• Events which occur that alter how students will respond to a typical situation.
• Situations which make it more likely that a problem behavior will occur or which make the behavior more intense. Skill deficits (poor reading skills) are an example.
• Setting events can be school based (a substitute teacher, a scheduled change of activities) or non-school based (health problems, inadequate sleep, medication issues, fight with parents in the morning before school, nutrition needs).

**Antecedents:**
• Events or circumstances, which happen before a behavior occurs that trigger the problem behavior.
• Antecedents will vary among students. An antecedent that sets off a problem behavior for one student can help another student perform successfully.
• Examples include: asking a student to complete a demanding task or transitions from one activity to another.

## Guiding Questions:
• In what settings do the behavior occur?
• What times of day are the behavior most and least likely to occur?
• Does the behavior occur in the presence of a certain person(s)?
• During which activities are the behavior most likely and least likely to occur?

**TIP:** It is just as important to look for antecedents that support a student's good behavior as it is to look for those that support inappropriate behavior. The former plays a crucial role in developing the BIP.

### Maintaining Consequences
• Things which occur immediately following the student's behavior, making it more likely that a behavior will occur again.
• Things which students find rewarding will increase a behavior.
• Sometimes consequences can actually reinforce the inappropriate behavior.

...continued on next page

## Step #6: Monitoring and Modifying the BIP

The team needs to monitor the student's problem, alternative and desired behaviors. It is often useful to utilize a Scatter Plot to monitor the BIP. This data should be compared to the baseline data (before BIP implementation) to evaluate whether the plan is working. Modifications to the plan should be based on this data. Graphing the data helps measure progress and determines the effectiveness of the plan.

• If the plan was implemented consistently, but progress toward goals was not achieved, additional assessment should be considered (return to Step # 2...Gathering Information)

• If the student has successfully achieved the desired behavior, the team should develop a maintenance plan to ensure continued success of the student while reducing the amount of staff time and resources.

## Web Resources

www.pbis.org
www.swis.org
www.apbs.org
www.successfulschools.com

## Print Resources

Crone, D. A. & Horner, R. H. (2015). *Building Positive Behavior Support Systems in Schools: Functional Behavioral Assessments, 2nd Edition.* New York, NY: Guilford Press.

Crone, D.A., Hawken, L.S. & Horner, R. H. (2010). *Responding to Problem Behavior in Schools, 2nd Ed.* New York, NY: Guilford Press.

O'Neill, R.E., Horner, R.H., Albin, R.W., Sprague, J.R., Storey, K., & Newton, J.S. (1997). *Functional Assessment and Program Development for Problem Behavior: A Practical Handbook.* Pacific Grove, CA: Brooks/Cole.

Quinn, M. M., Gable, R. A., Rutherford, R. B. Jr., Nelson, C. M., & Howell, K. (1998). *Addressing Student Problem Behavior: An IEP Team's Introduction to Functional Behavioral Assessment and Behavior Intervention Plans (2nd ed.).* Washington, D.C.: Center for Effective Collaboration and Practice.

Shore, K. (2010). *Classroom Management: A Guide for Elementary Teachers* (laminated reference guide). Port Chester, NY: Dude Publishing.

Steege, M. W. & Watson, T. S. (2009). *Conducting School-Based Functional Behavioral Assessments.* New York, NY: Guilford Press.

Wright, J. (2010). *RTI & Classroom Behaviors* (laminated reference guide). Port Chester, NY: Dude Publishing.

## The 6 Step FBA-BIP Process at a Quick Glance

**Step #1: Identifying and Defining the Problem Behaviors**
• Build a profile of the student's strengths and needs
• Develop a trans-disciplinary behavioral support team
• Define the problem behavior in observable and measurable terms

**Step #2: Gathering Information**
• Collect data using a collaborative process
• Indirect methods include: reviewing records and interviews
• Direct methods include an A-B-C Recording or a Scatter Plot

**Step #3: Generating a Summary Statement**
• A Behavior Summary Statement is a hypothesis which predicts the conditions under which the behavior is most likely to occur, and the probable consequences that maintain it
• Identify:
  ✓ <u>Setting events</u>: that set the stage for the behavior
  ✓ <u>Antecedents</u>: which are the events that occur immediately before the behavior (and set the behavior off)
  ✓ <u>Maintaining consequences</u>: which increase the likelihood that the behavior will occur again
  ✓ <u>Function of behavior</u>: which are strengthened or reinforced by the environment.

**Step #4: Developing a Behavior Intervention Plan (BIP)**
• Develop "antecedent" strategies as a proactive approach to prevent or mitigate the problem behavior
• Determine if the student has a skill deficit (Can't do) and/or a performance deficit (Won't do)
• Identify and teach the student alternative/replacement behaviors
• Modify consequences focusing on the use of positive reinforcement and changing the maintaining consequences

**Step #5: Implementing the BIP**
• Identify team members responsibilities in implementing the BIP
• Consistently implement the BIP and track all tasks

**Step #6: Monitoring and Modifying the BIP**
• The behavioral support team needs to monitor the student's behavior
• Compare the baseline data prior to the BIP implementation to the current behavior to measure progress and effectiveness
• Adjust the BIP as needed using additional assessment data
• Develop a maintenance plan if the BIP has achieved the desired behavior.

DUDE PUBLISHING

### Order From:

National Professional Resources, Inc.
**1-800-453-7461**
**www.NPRinc.com**
Item # FBAB

ISBN 978-1-935609-2
9 781935 609278